ROGER NIX

★ ★ ★ *president at* **6** ★ ★ ★

written by **NICK DAZÉ**

illustrated by **BILL ROBINSON**

three
bean press

Roger Nix, President at Six
Published by:
Three Bean Press, LLC
P.O. Box 301711
Jamaica Plain, MA 02130
info@threebeanpress.com • www.threebeanpress.com

Publishers Cataloging-in-Publication Data
Dazé, Nick
Roger Nix, President at Six / by Nick Dazé.
p. cm.
Summary: When a surly old man named Robert T. Plee announces he will run for president—which would mean the end of kids being kids—the confident kindergartner Roger Nix decides to take a stand and put his name on the ballot.

ISBN 978-0-9882212-1-5

[1. Children—Fiction. 2. Presidency—Fiction. 3. Elections—Fiction. 4. President—Fiction.]
I. Bill Robinson. II. Title.

LCCN 2012949153

Printed in the U.S.A. by Lifetouch through Four Colour Print Group, Louisville, Kentucky

10 9 8 7 6 5 4 3 2 1

This book is dedicated to the kids in Roger's kindergarten class:
Miles, Lucy, Matthew, Megan, Chris, and Andrew. Watching you grow
has been an inspiration—both for this book and for keeping my kid-ness.

There once was a boy who was boy-er than most.
He ate orange wedge pieces and cinnamon toast.
He was bold and adventurous. He liked playing catch.
He made people say, "Wow!" at the things he could sketch.

On the day he was born, he was named Roger Nix.
And he'd grown very smart by the time he was six.
He lived in a house with his mom and his pop.
His mom was a lawyer. His dad owned a shop.

Have you ever had an imaginary friend?
Well, Roger had *two* on whom he could depend:
An elephant, Abe, and a donkey named Jack.
Roger was head of their animal pack.

Their favorite game (they could play it for hours)
Was making believe that they had superpowers.
Or climbing Mount Everest (Jack was the winner),
Or swimming on Mars (they'd be home late for dinner).

Roger liked school. He loved kindergarten.
He liked his new teacher, Ms. Annabelle Dardenne.
She taught him his letters and numbers and shapes.
She put ninja bandages on gnarly knee scrapes.

One day after school there was late-breaking news.
All the people were watching their TVs for clues.
On came a man known as Robert T. Plee,
Who announced he would run for the presidency.

"Dear people who make this great country so grand:
Let's take back our nation, the time is at hand.
Let's mold these kids now, forget making them *scholars*.
We must teach them hard lessons, like the value of dollars!

No more show-and-tell and recess at school.
What do they take us for, silly old fools?
Kids eat crackers, drink juice. They make pots out of clay.
Tell me, what are they learning? They just *play all day!*"

(There's something to know about old Robert Plee:
Summed up in one word, he was quite "ornery.")
He was well reputed for dollars and sense.
Grown-ups liked that he never just "sat on the fence."

His plan was to close every school in his reaches
And put kids to work, canning cherries and peaches.

After hearing the news, Ms. Dardenne was teary,
Her nose was all pink, and her eyes were all bleary.
"Kids, we must think quickly of some way to act
Or our school will shut down—that is a fact."

Roger jumped to his feet.
He had something to say,
With a wink from Jack and
a trunks-up from Abe.

"*I'll* run against him," Roger said with a shout.
"*I'll* run for president—have you no doubt!

To close school would be nothing short of a crime.
You can't fool us kids, not *all* of the time."

He stood on his desk and they all watched and wondered.
As Roger kept talking, his voice boomed and thundered.

"We'll beat him and keep all the schools as they are,
Or make them way better. We'll shoot for the stars!
We go to school so one day we'll go far,
Not because it is easy—because it is *hard*!

We are KIDS! The whole point is to
learn and have fun
And to use our keen noggins....
THIS RACE HAS BEGUN!"

So Abe, Jack, and Roger got to work right away.
"The kid's on to something," his parents would say.
He made lots of speeches; he shook lots of hands;
He toured a big factory that made rubber bands.

Then one night on the tube, to Old Plee's disdain,
The news ran a story on Roger's campaign.
"Roger Nix, daydreamer and ultimate kid,
Is gaining on Plee in his presidential bid."

But everyone knew that sooner or later
Roger would have to be quite the debater.
Because in a short while, under some bright marquee,
A debate would take place between Roger and Plee.

When the two met each other
and came face to face,
They shook hand and finger,
and each took his place.
Old Man Plee towered tall,
almost tall as a bear,
Next to wee little Roger
(who stood on a chair).

The cameras that flashed were so bright that they stung,
While Mr. Plee bellowed these words from his tongue:

"Great people of this nation, this state, and this town,
You might hear a faint, whiny, childish sound.
Please try to stay focused—the sound will soon cease
When we cure Mr. Nix of his boyish disease.

The sickness I speak of, it squashes our pride.
It's the illness of children expecting free rides.
It's time that they work, like us normal adults.
We'll shut down the schools, then we'll see some results.

We work through their summer and winter vacations,
Alone, We, the grown-ups are building this nation!

Adults of the land, *don't you see the potential?*
Our kids are an untapped work force, essential.
If we gave them all jobs, in just a short time,
Our economy will run at its peak—at its prime."

A thund'rous applause rang out through the hall,
Plee thought that he had Roger's back to the wall.

When the roar simmered down, they turned their attention
To Roger, who gulped with great apprehension.
Jack nudged him gently behind his left knee,
And Abe said, "Speak softly, and *beat Robert Plee*."

He took a deep breath. He said a quick prayer.
Then he stated his case with passion and flair:

"Kids need their KID-ness, and summer vacation,
And cool superheroes with awesome mutations!
They need paste and paper and cardboard juice boxes.
They *need* dogs and worm guts and striped baseball soxes.

They need, most of all, their imaginations.
Let grown-ups concern about jobs and bus stations,
And traffic and stock markets, 401(k)s...
If that's how a grown-up spends his or her days.

Because, as you know, kids turn into teens.
And teens go to college and come out Marines
And doctors and shoeshines. Adults, every one.

How can you de-kid your daughters and sons?"

Plee countered, "This kid sits around and relaxes,
He should go find a job, earn some money, pay taxes.
And may I remind you, not *all* kids are wasters—
I worked as a youngster, delivering papers!"

From the cheering adults in their scarves and their coats,
There came a cracked-creaky: "Oh no, no you don't."

It was ever so feeble yet had quite a purpose.
It came from a woman all hat, specs, and purses.
Then again, she repeated more definitely,
"Oh no, no you don't, Robert Theodore Plee!"

The crowd hushed and they parted. An old lady stood,
Hunched, frail, and aged, with a cane made of wood.

Many whispers and murmurs spread all through the crowd.
"She looks ninety-three," they said, slightly too loud.

"Ninety-SIX," corrected this little old lady.
"Ninety-six, and I don't look a day over eighty!"

This woman made sure they could hear in the lobby,
As she faced Old Man Plee and called him "My Bobby."
"Mother?" said Plee, with confusion and fear,
"What are you... How are you... Why are you here?"

She pulled out a picture, which she waved about proudly.
"My son was a boy once!" she said very loudly.

The old snapshot pictured a young Old Man Plee.
He was missing a tooth and had dirt on his knee.
He sat at a booth selling fresh lemonade,
While reading some comics with pages all frayed.

"My boy never came in for dinner on time.
He'd be out playing stickball—he'd find trees to climb.
He'd spend every weekend exploring the woods.
And we let him. We thought it would do him some good."

Growing chatter and nods rippled all through the crowd,
It was like Mother Plee had just lifted a cloud.
The people looked 'round and remembered together
That they were once kids. (And they'd liked that time better.)

Roger noted the mood and seized that very minute
To drive his point home—this is where he could win it.
He pitched his campaign with fervor and might,
His platform of goodness and kid-ness and rights.

The next day, two words were on everyone's lips:
The first word was "Roger," the second was "Nix."

Election Day came, all the pollsters could see
That everyone voted, but not for Old Plee.
They voted for Roger to show them the way,
To show them it's okay to laugh, learn, and play

So Roger, age six, became President Nix.
He put things in order, like laying down bricks.
Though young, he was earnest in office and oath
And made proper choices that brought about growth.

He kept the schools open in winter and spring,
And reminded adults 'bout "that childhood thing."
Because Roger was kind and because he was good,
In history, his legend unshakably stood.

The moral of the story tells all that there is:
Imagination is what we must learn from our kids.
From there they will go wherever they will,
Mount Everest or Mars—even Capitol Hill.